CW00495794

MASTE.
NINTENDO S
COMPLETE GUIDE TO
GAMING EXCELLENCE

Unleash the Power of Your Console with
Setup Tips, Advanced Strategies, and
Exclusive Insights

Joshua Talbot

Copyright © 2024 By Joshua Talbot

TABLE OF CONTENTS

INTRODUCTION

Greetings and welcome to the comprehensive guide for your Nintendo Switch—your doorway to a world of limitless gaming options! This book is your key to releasing the full potential of the Switch, regardless of how experienced you are as a player or how recently you acquired it. Explore the upcoming chapters to learn everything you need to know to maximise your gaming experience, from basic setup to sophisticated advice. Prepare yourself to travel through the Nintendo Switch's features, add-ons, and fascinating world. Now let's get the adventure started!

GETTING YOUR NINTENDO SWITCH STARTED

Enter the Nintendo Switch universe, where endless gaming opportunities lie ahead. This section serves as your entry point to the console's essential features, covering anything from basic setup procedures to simple controller connectivity. Come along with us as we clarify the first steps and open the door for your Switch journey.

Configuring Your Console

It's simple but important to set up your Nintendo Switch for a flawless gaming experience. To get your console operating, adhere to these comprehensive instructions:

1. Opening the Box and First Examining:
Make sure every part of your Nintendo Switch is there before taking it out of the box.
Check for any obvious damage on the console, dock, Joy-Cons, Joy-Con grip, HDMI cable, and power adapter.

2. Dock Connectivity:
Keep the Nintendo Switch dock close to your monitor or TV.
Using the included power adapter, connect the dock to a power source.
Make sure the opposite end of the HDMI cable is plugged into your TV or monitor before attaching it to the dock.

3. Switching on:

Insert the Nintendo Switch system into the docking station.

Press the power button on the top-left side of the console to turn it on.

To choose your language, region, and other initial options, adhere to the on-screen instructions.

4. Combining Joy-Cons:

Press the release buttons located on the rear of the Joy-Cons to separate them from the console.

Each Joy-Con's sync button should be held down until the lights begin to flash.

To pair the Joy-Cons with the console, follow the on-screen instructions.

5. Establishing a Nintendo Account or Linking One:

Make a Nintendo Account using a web browser or the console if you don't already have one.

Sign in to your existing account to link it to your Nintendo Switch.

6. Updates for the system:

To check for system updates, connect your Switch to the internet.

To guarantee that your console is running the most recent firmware, download and install any updates that are available.

7. Configuring Wireless Internet:
Go to the Home menu and select System Settings.
Select "Internet" and choose your Wi-Fi network, entering the needed password.

8. User Characteristics:
Choose "Add Friend" from the home menu to create user profiles for every player.
Customise each profile with a nickname and Mii.

Linking Controllers and Joy-Cons

Linking Joy-Cons and other controllers to your Nintendo Switch expands your multiplayer options and improves gaming. Here's a comprehensive how-to for smoothly integrating these input devices:

1. Using the Console to Attach the Joy-Cons:
Slide the Joy-Cons onto the console's side rails until you hear a click to start playing in handheld mode.
Make sure the Joy-Cons' "+" and "-" buttons line up with the relevant symbols on the console.

2. Removing Joy-Cons for Single- or Multiplayer Gaming:
To detach, slide each Joy-Con upward while holding the release button on the rear of the device.
For games like Mario Kart, use them separately; alternatively, attach them to the Joy-Con grip for a more conventional controller experience.

3. Wireless Joy-Con Pairing:
Go to System Settings from the home menu.
Choose "Controllers and Sensors" and then "Change Grip/Order."

Each Joy-Con's sync button should be held down until the lights begin to flash.
Select "Pair New Controllers" from the menu, then adhere to the prompts.

4. How to Use the Joy-Con Grip

To combine the separated Joy-Cons into a single controller, just slide them into the Joy-Con grasp.
To charge the grip, attach the USB cable to the console.

5. Linking Up Extra Controllers:

The procedure for gaining access to "Change Grip/Order" in the System Settings and syncing additional controllers—like Pro Controllers—remains the same.

6. Linking Bluetooth controllers:

Bluetooth communication is supported by certain third-party controllers.
Activate Bluetooth on the console via System Preferences and adhere to the pairing guidelines provided by the controller.

7. Fixing Problems with Connections:

Make sure the controllers are charged if they aren't connecting.

Try pairing the console once more after power cycling it.

Verify whether any other electronic gadgets are interfering.

8. Changing the Controller's Settings:

To change the sensitivity of buttons and other settings, go to the "Controllers and Sensors" section of System Settings.

9. Modes for multiplayer:

Connect many controllers to enjoy local multiplayer.

To get the most out of your multiplayer experience, check out the settings as some games enable multiple control methods.

NAVIGATING THE INTERFACE

Embark on a trip through the intuitive UI of the Nintendo Switch. This part covers how to use the Home Menu, download games from the eShop, and find the fluid controls that enhance the immersiveness of your gameplay. Let's dissect the UI to make each menu and setting simple to reach so you can enjoy playing the game.

Overview of the Home Menu

Your Nintendo Switch's Home Menu is its major hub, offering easy access to settings, games, and other apps. Your entire navigation experience is improved by being aware of its characteristics. Here's a detailed summary:

1. Classic Design:
A grid of square icons that symbolise various apps and games may be found in the Home Menu.
The Album for screenshots, the News section for updates, and the eShop for game purchases are essential components.

2. Quick Launch and Gaming Tiles:
On the Home Menu, recent or frequently played games are displayed as huge tiles.
Press "A" after selecting a game tile to start the game immediately.

3. User Info and List of Friends:
Your Mii and user settings are easily accessible thanks to the conspicuous display of your user profile symbol.

You may check friend requests, view who's online, and access friend-related functions by clicking the Friend List icon.

4. Configuration of the System:
Access to the System Settings through the gear-shaped icon lets you adjust several console parameters.
To make the Switch your own, change the user settings, display, sound, and internet.

5. News Feed:
Use the News area to stay up to date on the most recent news and game releases.
Receive alerts regarding system news, in-game happenings, and software changes.

6. Record & Recording:
Holding down the Capture button on the left Joy-Con records video clips and takes screenshots.
To see and organise the media you've captured, go to the Album.

7. Supervisors:
Via the Controllers icon, pair new controllers and verify the connected controllers' battery condition.

8. eShop:

Browse the Nintendo eShop's selection of games and other downloadable items and buy it.

Watch sales, previews, and new product releases on the dynamic eShop interface.

9. Internet-based Services:

Use the Online Services icon to access your Nintendo Switch Online subscription.

Handle your subscription, play NES/SNES games, and play multiplayer online.

10. Alerts:

Notifications about new friend requests, messages, and other system events are displayed through the envelope symbol.

11. Mode of Sleep:

Press the power button to quickly enter Sleep Mode on your console, which enables you to start playing again right away.

12. Personalisation:

You can rearrange and organise your games and programmes by holding down on a tile to customise the layout of your Home Menu.

Using the eShop for Downloads

Your digital doorway to a huge selection of games, trailers, and extra material for your Nintendo Switch is the Nintendo eShop. Here's a detailed tutorial to help you get the most out of the eShop and navigate it for smooth downloads:

1. Getting into the eShop:
To access the digital storefront, open the Nintendo Switch Home Menu and choose the eShop icon.

2. Looking through the Shop:
On the home screen, have a look at the highlighted games, ongoing offers, and recent releases.
Browse a selection of titles by navigating through categories such as Deals, Recent Releases, and Best Sellers.

3. Information and Specifics of the Game:
To view a game's details page, click on its icon.
Discover details about the game, system requirements, user reviews, screenshots, and videos.

4. Buying Video Games:

To purchase a game, select "Proceed to Purchase". Before paying, select whether to buy the entire game or a demo (if available).

5. Options for Payment:
You can use a credit card, PayPal, or a Nintendo eShop gift card to add money to your Nintendo eShop account.
Support for secure transactions guarantees a secure shopping experience.

6. Installing and downloading games:
Choose "Download" to start the download and installation process after making a purchase.
Games that have finished downloading will appear on your Home Menu.

7. DLC, or downloadable content
Use the eShop to get access to more game content, including expansions, outfits, and in-game goods.
DLC can be downloaded and purchased to improve your gaming.

8. Free Samples:
Try out games before purchasing by downloading free demos from the eShop.

Demos give you a taste of the action and assist you in determining whether or not a game is right for you.

9. Desired List:

Make a wish list of the games you want to play so you can easily find and buy them later.

Receive notifications when wish-listed games become on sale.

10. Pre-load and Pre-purchase:

You can pre-purchase some games prior to their release date.

With pre-load, you can download the game in advance and start playing it as soon as it's released.

11. Updates and Upkeep for eShops:

The eShop is updated frequently with new games, deals, and promotions.

Recognise when maintenance is scheduled to prevent disruptions while downloading.

12. How to Redeem Download Codes

To redeem digital copies through the eShop, enter download codes that you received from promotions or physical game purchases.

UTILISING YOUR SWITCH FOR GAMING

Take a deep dive into the vibrant world of gaming with us as we explore how to play games on your Nintendo Switch. This section reveals all the several ways you can play a large library of games, from the satisfying tactile experience of putting in game cards to the easy organisation of your digital libraries. Allow the excitement of gaming to take you to a world of limitless entertainment options.

Inserting and Removing Game Cards on Your Nintendo Switch:

Putting the Game Cards in:

1. Find the Slot for the Game Card:
The Nintendo Switch console's top is where the Game Card slot is situated.
Before putting in or taking out game cards, make sure the console is turned off or in sleep mode.

2. Place the game card in the appropriate position.
With the label facing you, hold the game card.
Make sure the golden contacts on the Game Card line up with the contacts within the slot as you align it with the slot.

3. Place the game card in gently:
Once the Game Card snaps into position, slide it into the slot.
Keep your force to a minimum; the card should go in easily.

4. Turn on and begin playing:

The game icon will show up on the Home Menu when the Nintendo Switch is powered on.
Click the icon of the game to begin.

Taking Out the Game Cards:

1. Make sure the console is in sleep mode or is powered off:
Verify that no games are currently playing on the console before removing a game card.

2. Find the "Eject" button.
The small, rectangular Eject button is located on the top-left side of the console.

3. Push the button to eject:
Partially remove the Game Card from the slot by gently pressing the Eject button.

4. Take out the game card:
Take the Game Card out of the slot by holding it by its edges.
Take care not to come into contact with the Game Card's bottom contacts.

5. How to Store Game Cards Safely:

24

To avoid damage, put the removed game card in either the original game case or a protective one.

Advice on Maintaining Game Cards:

- Avoid Forceful Removal: Never take a game card out of its case by force. Verify sure the console is either powered off or in sleep mode if it doesn't eject readily.
- Properly Store: To avoid scuffs and damage, keep game cards in their protective cases.
- Examine Game Cards: Check each game card for any obvious damage before placing it. Steer clear of faulty cards to avoid console problems.

Managing the Digital Game Collection on Your Nintendo Switch:

On the Nintendo Switch, effective administration becomes crucial for a flawless gaming experience as your library of digital titles expands. This is a thorough how-to for managing the content in your digital game library:

1. Organising a Home Menu:
Your most recent games are prominently displayed on the Home Menu.
Navigate the horizontal list to locate and open the titles you've recently played.

2. Section for All Software:
To see all of the installed games in alphabetical order, navigate to the "All Software" area of the Home Menu.
Navigate the list to swiftly find particular titles.

3. Personalised Folders:
To arrange games according to genres, categories, or personal tastes, create custom folders.

Tap a game icon, choose "Add to a group," then either create a new folder or select one that already exists.

4. Information and Icons for Games:
Game icons make it simple to recognise games that are played frequently by displaying information like playtime.
To view further details, such as the status of updates and the downloadable content (DLC) that is available, select one of the game's icons.

5. Options for Sorting:
Sort games by alphabetical order, playtime, or most recent play by using the sorting options found in the "All Software" section.
This function makes it easier to find specific titles in a huge library rapidly.

6. Redownloading video games:
Visit the Nintendo eShop if you wish to play a digital game again after deleting it.
Go to your account, choose "Redownload," and get the games you've already bought.

7. SD Card Administration:

If you need more room and your console's internal storage is getting low, you might want to use a microSD card.

Using the System Settings, move games between the microSD card and internal storage.

8. Unused Games in the Archive:

Store games you don't play often in an archive to clear up space on the internal storage.

When you archive a game, the save data is kept intact, so you can reinstall it and play it at a later time.

9. Updates for software:

To make sure your games are running the most recent versions, be sure to frequently check for updates under the "All Software" area.

For ease of use, turn on automatic updates in the System Settings.

10. Parental Restraints:

Use the Parental Controls feature to carefully manage your digital library.

For younger users, impose limits on their playtime, purchases, and online interactions.

11. Cloud Savings

Cloud saving can be enabled by subscribing to Nintendo Switch Online.

Make a cloud backup of your save data to safeguard your gaming progress.

FEATURES FOR ONLINE AND MULTIPLAYER GAMING

Take use of your Nintendo Switch to explore the thrilling world of online and multiplayer gaming, where the single-player game experience is enhanced. This part explores the social aspects of your console by walking you through the process of setting up local multiplayer games, establishing online connections with friends, and exploring the endless possibilities of both competitive and cooperative gameplay. As we discover the vast array of online and multiplayer capabilities, let the virtual friendships start, transforming every game session into a shared journey.

Getting Nintendo Switch Local Multiplayer Set Up:

Using the Nintendo Switch's local multiplayer feature, families and friends may enjoy a shared gaming experience. It's easy to set up local multiplayer for cooperative exploration or competitive warfare. Here's a how-to manual to get you going:

1. Ascertain Adequate Controllers:
Ensure that there are enough controllers for every player taking part in the local multiplayer game.
Joy-Cons, Pro Controllers, and other controllers that are compatible can be used for this.

2. Locate and select the Home Menu:
Choose the game you wish to play in local multiplayer from the Home Menu.
Make sure the game allows for local multiplayer; many well-known games do.

3. Get to the multiplayer modes:
Look for choices or multiplayer modes on the game's main menu.

Certain games may feature dedicated party modes or multiplayer portions.

4. Select the Amount of Players:
Decide how many people are taking part in the local multiplayer game.
Depending on the game, options for two, four, or more players are frequently offered.

5. Assign the Controllers:
Assign controllers to each player by following on-screen directions.
Press particular buttons on the controllers to associate them with particular characters in the game, for instance.

6. Adapt the Settings as Necessary:
You can change certain game parameters, like match length, team compositions, and difficulty levels.
To start the game, change these settings to your preferred level of difficulty.

7. Launch the multiplayer session locally:
After assigning controllers and modifying the parameters, start the local multiplayer game.

All of the chosen players will be able to play when the game loads.

8. Have Fun with the Game:
Play through the chosen multiplayer options while collaborating or competing with pals.
Friendly rivalry and teamwork are fostered by the lively and social gaming experience that local multiplayer offers.

9. Conclude the Meeting:
Go back to the main menu of the game when you're done playing.
You have the option to end the multiplayer game, pick a different mode, or play another round.

Advice for Local Multiplayer:
- Verify the game's compatibility before playing it to make sure local multiplayer is supported.
- Try Different Controller Configurations: Depending on the game, you may find that certain configurations or control schemes work better for your style of play.

- Charge Controllers: Prior to beginning a local multiplayer game, make sure all controllers are sufficiently charged.

Exploring Online Services on Your Nintendo Switch

Nintendo Switch Online services provide access to a world of multiplayer online games, special offers, and other features. This thorough guide will assist you in exploring and utilising the Nintendo Switch's internet services to the fullest:

1. Nintendo Switch Subscription Online:
A Nintendo Switch Online subscription is required in order to access online services.
For single or family plans, subscribe via the Nintendo website or eShop.

2. Configuring the Nintendo Switch for Internet play:
After subscribing, access the Switch's System Settings.
Choose "Nintendo Switch Online" by scrolling down to create an online profile.

3. Playing multiplayer video games online:
Enjoy engaging in online multiplayer gaming with friends or people all around the world.

In the eShop, find out which of your favourite games are compatible with online multiplayer.

4. Voice Chat and Interaction:
If you want to voice chat while playing online, use the Nintendo Switch Online app on your smartphone.
Interact with teammates and friends to improve the multiplayer experience.

5. Exclusive NES/SNES Game Access:
Classic NES and SNES games are available to play on Nintendo Switch Online.
Play these timeless games to relive the good times or introduce them to a younger audience.

6. Save Data on the Cloud:
Use cloud save data to safeguard your gaming progress.
You can recover your game data by connecting to a new device in the event that your console is broken or lost.

7. Online Competitions and Events:
Take part in Nintendo-hosted online competitions and events.

Compete with players worldwide and get rewards for your efforts.

8. Exclusive Deals and Savings:
Subscribers to Nintendo Switch Online frequently receive exclusive deals and discounts.
Watch the eShop for exclusive offers on games and DLC.

9. Parental Guidelines for Internet Gaming:
Make use of the Parental Controls function to supervise younger users' internet activities.
To create a secure gaming environment, impose limitations on internet functions and communication.

10. Web-based mobile application:
On your smartphone, download the Nintendo Switch Online app.
You may check online play statistics, access unique content, and have audio chats with it.

11. Controllers for SNES/NES:
Get the SNES or NES wireless controllers that are compatible with Nintendo Switch Online.

These controllers provide a nostalgic experience for vintage video games.

12. Keep Up with Service Improvements:
Nintendo improves and refreshes the Nintendo Switch Online service on a regular basis.
Keep yourself updated on service enhancements, additions, and new features.

GETTING THE MOST OUT OF YOUR GAMING EXPERIENCE

By learning how to maximise your gaming experience, you can make the most of your Nintendo Switch adventure. This section reveals the various ways you can customise your console settings, improve the look and feel, and simplify the controls to suit your tastes. Come help us customise every element of your gaming environment, from system setups to making sure parental controls suit your family's needs. Let's examine the capabilities and tools that turn your Nintendo Switch into a customised gaming paradise.

Changing the Nintendo Switch's System Settings:

You may customise your Nintendo Switch to fit your tastes by changing the system settings, which guarantees a unique and enjoyable gaming experience. Here's a thorough tutorial on experimenting with and modifying different settings:

1. Getting to the System Preferences:
Find and pick the "System Settings" gear-shaped icon from the Home Menu.

2. Theme and Colour Configurations:
Select a theme to give your Switch a unique appearance.
In the "Themes" area, change the theme, brightness, and colour palette.

3. Configuration of the User:
In the "Users" section, you can link or unlink Nintendo Accounts, manage user profiles, and Mii characters.
Personalised user settings provide for a more customised experience.

4. Configuring the Console Battery:

Under the "Console Battery" section, keep an eye on and control battery usage.

To get precise battery level alerts or to optimise battery life, adjust the parameters.

5. Configuration of the Sleep Mode:

You can adjust the Sleep Mode settings to manage when your Switch goes into low power.

In the System Settings, go to "Sleep Mode" and modify the sleep schedule and other settings.

6. Brightness of the Screen:

In the "Screen Brightness" area, adjust the screen brightness for tabletop and handheld modes.

Determine the ideal ratio between battery life and visibility.

7. Configuring the Internet:

In the "Internet" area, connect to Wi-Fi networks, adjust network settings, and resolve connectivity problems.

To access online features and game updates, keep your Switch connected.

8. Sensors and Controllers:

Adjust the controller's settings, such as the sensitivity and button configurations.

In the "Controllers and Sensors" section, calibrate controllers and oversee associated devices.

9. Alerts:

In the "Notifications" section, you may manage notifications for friend requests, messages, and other system updates.

Modify your notification preferences to reduce disruptions while playing.

10. Information Administration:

The "Data Management" part is where you manage applications and store data.

Eliminate extraneous information or move files to a microSD card to make room.

11. Update for the System:

Check for system updates on a regular basis to keep your console current.

To ensure easy access to the newest features and enhancements, enable automatic updates.

12. Parental Restraints:

To govern online interactions, limit playtime, and prevent access to specific services, set up and monitor parental controls.

Make sure that each user profile has settings that are appropriate for their age.

13. Language and Region Settings:

In the "System" section, change your preferred language and region.

Play games and access content that are region-specific.

Using Nintendo Switch's Parental Controls:

With the Nintendo Switch's Parental Controls, you can keep a close eye on your child's gaming activities and provide a secure, age-appropriate environment. This is a thorough guide that will show you how to use parental controls:

1. Configuring Parental Regulators:
Open the Nintendo Switch's System Settings.
To start the setting procedure, scroll down to "Parental Controls" and choose "Use this feature".

2. Establishing a PIN for Parental Controls:
Select a PIN that will be needed to get access to and alter the Parental Controls configuration.
To keep control over the settings, keep the PIN private.

3. Limiting the Play Time:
Establish daily or weekly limitations to help you manage your child's playtime.
When the playtime restriction is about to expire, the console will alert your child.

4. Levels of Content Restriction:
Customise content limitations based on your child's age and maturity level.
Modify the settings to limit the use of apps, gaming, and internet messaging.

5. Limiting Features of Communication:
Limit communication tools to manage relationships with friends and other gamers.
Manage friend requests, communications, and the option to submit screenshots on social media.

6. Activating Limitations on Web Browsers:
You can limit your child's access to the web browser within the Nintendo Switch Online app.

7. Observing the Play:
See comprehensive play activity records for your child, including with playtime duration and titles played.
To maintain equilibrium, keep yourself updated about your child's gaming habits.

8. Remote Control through Application:
On your smartphone, download the Nintendo Switch Parental Controls app.
Set play time limits, monitor play activities, and get remote notifications using this app.

9. Short-Term Pauses:
Use temporary suspensions to put a stop to your gaming rights for a predetermined amount of time.
useful for handling behavioural issues or imposing breaks.

10. Changing the PIN Settings:
Modify or reset the Parental Controls PIN, as well as temporarily disable the feature, by adjusting its associated settings.

11. Override for emergencies:
You can temporarily lift limitations using the Parental Controls PIN in the event of an emergency or unanticipated occurrence.

12. For the Nintendo eShop, parental controls:
Limit the amount of digital content you can buy from the Nintendo eShop.

Make sure your youngster never purchases anything without your consent.

SOCIAL & COMMUNITY VIDEO GAMES

Take a deep dive into the colourful world of social gaming and community on your Nintendo Switch. This area serves as your entry point for interacting with other players, making allies, and going on joint adventures. Learn about the subtleties of friend codes, delve into the realm of virtual communities, and optimise social functionalities. Come along as we explore the social aspects of gaming and show you how to use your Nintendo Switch as a gateway to friendship and shared experiences. Let the community thrive as we explore into the exciting realm of social gaming.

Using Nintendo Switch Friend Codes and Friend Requests:

Nintendo Switch has an exclusive feature called Friend Codes to let users interact with each other. Your social gaming experience is improved if you know how to handle friend requests and trade friend codes. Here's a thorough guide:

1. Finding Your Code of Friendship:
From the Home Menu, you may access your profile. There is a 12-digit combination on the screen that is Your Friend Code.

2. Giving Out Your Friend Code:
If you wish to connect with friends or acquaintances, give them your Friend Code.
It can be distributed by text messaging, social media, or other methods of communication.

3. Requesting Friendships:
To send a friend request, check your friend's profile or enter their Friend Code directly.
Select "Send Friend Request" and bide your time for their acceptance.

4. Taking in Requests for Friends:

Your Home Menu will notify you when you receive a friend request.

Locate the pending request on the Friend List, select it, then decide whether to accept or reject it.

5. Friend List Administration:

To see the status of friend requests and your existing friends, go to your friend list.

For simpler administration, classify your friends or form groups.

6. Feature of Best Friends:

Assign specific individuals to be your "Best Friends" to receive extra perks.

Best Friends may send direct messages, join your games without an invitation, and know when you're online.

7. Play Multiplayer Online and Locally with Friends:

You can invite friends to play games with you or take part in local multiplayer sessions once they've been added.

Certain games additionally provide elements that are unique to online multiplayer gaming.

8. Speaking with Pals:

Text and voice chat with pals using the Nintendo Switch Online app.

Directly send your pals updates, game highlights, and screenshots.

9. Eliminating Pals:

You can take pals off your list if necessary.

You can undo this action at any time and add them again later if you'd like.

10. Recommendations from friends:

Get recommendations for possible companions based on shared interests and games you've recently played.

Examine these ideas to grow your gaming community.

11. Friend features specific to a game:

There are particular friend features in some games.

Examine friend lists, guilds, and other community features specific to the game.

Joining and Creating Nintendo Switch Gaming Communities:

On the Nintendo Switch, gaming communities offer a venue for similar players to meet, exchange stories, and plan group play sessions. Here's a guide to adjusting to this social side of gaming, whether you wish to join already-existing communities or start your own:

1. Acquiring Membership in Pre-existing Communities:
Examine the "User Page" of any online buddies or players you come across.
There are players whose profiles are connected to communities.
If a community appeals to your gaming interests, ask to join it.

2. Getting to the User Page:
By choosing a player's profile from your friend list or recently played players, you can get to the User Page.
To learn more about their communities, go to the "Friend Settings" area.

3. Integrating into Private and Public Communities:
While some communities might be private and require an invitation to join, others might be public and open to everyone.
Send a request to the community owner to gain access to private communities.

4. Nintendo Switch Web App:
To access and administer communities, use the Nintendo Switch Online software on your mobile device.
Get alerts, participate in conversations, and plan game sessions while on the road.

5. Taking Part in Conversations in the Community:
Participate in community discussions and exchange gaming experiences, tactics, and advice.
Keep up with local happenings and online gaming sessions.

6. Building Your Own Group:
Go to your profile, then click on "User Page."
To start a new community, select "Create a Friend Room" from the "Friend Settings" menu by scrolling down.

7. Personalising Community Information:
Give your community a name, establish privacy settings, and outline its goals.
To make your community stand out, personalise the banners, emblems, and other elements.

8. Greeting Friends in Your Neighbourhood:
Send a direct invitation to friends so they can join your community.
For wider access, select particular pals or make your community public.

9. Taking Care of Community Participants:
You have the power to oversee members as the community's owner.
Members can be added or removed, and community settings can be changed as needed.

10. Events and Announcements:
Use the announcement section of the community to communicate significant developments and forthcoming events.
Arrange competitions or multiplayer sessions with other community members.

11. Breaking Up a Community:

A community can be dissolved if you decide you no longer want to maintain it.

Please take note that the community will be removed and that this action is irreversible.

12. Notifying Us About Unsuitable Content:

Use the reporting tools provided to report any offensive behaviour or content inside a community.

Contribute to keeping the game atmosphere welcoming and upbeat.

ADD-ONS AND IMPROVEMENTS

Set out on a quest to improve your Nintendo Switch experience by exploring the world of add-ons and accessories. This section serves as your guide to maximising the capabilities of your console, from increasing storage for your expanding collection to improving comfort during prolonged gaming sessions. Explore a world of remote controls, cases, and accessories that protect and improve your device. Let's examine the numerous add-ons that elevate your Nintendo Switch from a customisable gaming machine to an elegant, comfortable, and useful addition to your gaming experiences.

Examining Compatible Nintendo Switch Accessories:

Enjoy your Nintendo Switch experience to the fullest with a variety of accessories made to protect your console, increase comfort, and improve gaming. These compatible attachments provide flexibility and personalisation whether you're at home or on the go. Now let's explore the world of gaming accessories that can enhance your gaming experiences:

1. Supervisors:
Cons: Adaptable detachable controllers that can be used for docked, tabletop, or handheld play.
Pro Controller: An improved feature-rich classic style controller designed for comfortable gaming sessions.

2. Grip Add-ons:
Joy-Con Grip: Transforms your Joy-Cons into a more classic controller shape for enhanced comfort.
Pro Grip: Enhances the grip and feel of the Pro Controller, responding to individual tastes.

3. Solutions for Charging:

Dock Charger: By docking numerous Joy-Cons into a charging station, you can charge them all at once.

Multiple Pro Controllers may be conveniently charged in a single station with the Pro Controller Charging station.

4. Keeping Cases Alive:

Hard Shell Case: Offers your Nintendo Switch strong protection when travelling.

Carrying Pouch: A portable, lightweight solution for on-the-go Switch carrying.

5. Screen shields:

Tempered Glass Protectors: Prevent dents and scratches on your Switch's screen.

Film shields: Thin and easy-to-apply shields enabling scratch resistance.

6. Extension of Memory:

microSD Cards: Increase the storage space on your console to accommodate additional game downloads and entertainment.

7. Mounts and Stands:

Adjustable stands: By changing the viewing angle for more comfortable play, you may improve tabletop gaming.

Wall Mounts: For a distinctive display option, mount your switch to the wall.

8. Headgear and Audio Add-ons:

Gaming Headsets: For a more engaging experience, submerge yourself in the sound of your preferred games.

Bluetooth adapters: To enjoy a wide range of audio options, pair wireless headphones.

9. Docks and Connectors:

Portable Docks: Condensed options for charging and docking when travelling.

LAN Adapters: A connected internet connection enhances online connectivity.

10. Accessories for gaming:

Amiibo: Interactive figurines that improve Nintendo Switch game play in a variety of games.

Nintendo Labo Kits: DIY kits that mix physical and digital game experiences.

11. Accessory Personalisation:

Skin Decals: Adhesive skins in a variety of designs allow you to customise your Switch.

Thumb Grips: With customised thumb grips, you can increase comfort and control accuracy.

12. Power Banks:

Portable Chargers: Use a power bank to recharge your Switch to prolong your gaming sessions while on the go.

13. Joy-Con Add-ons:

Attachable wrist straps known as joy-cons provide a firm grip for playing motion-controlled video games.

Joy-Con Charging Grip: combines the charging capabilities of Joy-Cons with the usefulness of a grip.

Increasing Storage Capacity and Increasing Nintendo Switch Battery Life:

Upgrading storage and maximising battery life become crucial for a seamless gaming experience as your Nintendo Switch library grows. Here's a how-to for increasing battery life and storage capacity:

1. Enhancing Storage Capabilities:
microSD Cards: Use a high-capacity microSD card to expand the storage on your Switch.
Compatibility: Select microSD cards in 32GB to 1TB capacities, based on your requirements.

2. How to Insert a MicroSD Card
Find the microSD Card Slot on the back of the Switch; it's under the kickstand.
Insert the Card: Press the card into the slot with gentle pressure until it clicks into place.

3. Data Transfer:
System Settings: Open System Settings and find the "Data Management" option.

Move Data: Move videos and games from the microSD card to the internal storage.

4. Selecting Correct microSD Card:
Choose a microSD card with a high speed class if you want to read and write data more quickly.
Nintendo-Licensed Cards: For best results, Nintendo suggests using certain licenced microSD cards.

5. Keeping an eye on storage:
Verify Storage Space: To prevent running out of space, check your storage space on a regular basis under the System Settings.
Delete Extraneous Data: To make room, remove any games or data that you no longer require.

6. Increasing Battery Life:
Reduce the brightness of the screen in order to save battery life.
Turn Off HD Rumble: To save battery life, turn off HD Rumble in the System Preferences.

7. Turning on the aeroplane mode
System Preferences: To disconnect from Wi-Fi and save energy, turn on Aeroplane Mode.

Play while the Switch is charging to extend its battery life when playing for longer periods of time.

8. Software Updates:

System Updates: To maximise performance, keep the newest system software on your Switch up to date.

Update your games to take advantage of the performance improvements made by developers.

9. Employing External Power Sources:

Carry a large-capacity power bank with you for convenient on-the-go charging.

When charging a Switch, make sure to use USB Type-C cords to ensure compatibility.

10. Examining the Health of the Battery:

Battery Health Section: Check the condition of your battery in the System Preferences.

Replace If Necessary: You should think about getting a new battery if the condition of the old one drastically deteriorates.

11. Making Use of Energy-Sparing Features

Turn on Auto-Sleep in the System Preferences to make the Switch go to sleep on its own when not in use.

Optimise Settings: Depending on your preferences, change the settings for features that use a lot of power.

ADVANCED FEATURES AND TIPS

Venture into the world of sophisticated features and tricks, where the Nintendo Switch experience goes beyond the fundamentals. This area reveals secret features, pro techniques, and insider knowledge to help you get the most out of your console. Come along on an adventure to improve your gaming skills, from learning how to use sophisticated controls to discovering hidden features. Together, we will explore the nuances of your Nintendo Switch and uncover a wealth of knowledge and strategies that will turn your gaming sessions into unmatched journeys. Greetings from the world of advanced features and tips, where each play turns into a mastery and each tip opens up new possibilities.

Nintendo Switch Screenshots and Video Capture Expertise:

By becoming proficient with your Nintendo Switch's screenshot and video capture tools, you can unleash the potential of visual storytelling. Enhance your gaming experience by capturing unforgettable moments, preserving great moments, and even sharing your victories with other gamers. Here's a thorough how-to to maximise these features:

1. Taking Images of Screens:
Capture Button: To quickly take a screenshot, press the square-shaped Capture Button on the left Joy-Con or the Pro Controller.
Album: From the Home Menu, select the Album to view your screenshots.

2. Taking Pictures using a Handheld Device:
Power + Volume Down: To take screenshots in handheld mode, simultaneously press the Power and Volume Down keys.
Album Access: To view captures made in handheld mode, open the Album from the Home Menu.

3. Taking Video Clips:

Hold Capture Button: To record a video of the previous 30 seconds of gameplay, hold down the Capture Button.

Editing Videos: To bring attention to the most thrilling parts, cut and edit the video segments in the album.

4. Changing the Capture Settings:

Adjust the capture parameters in the System Settings by going to "Data Management" and then "Manage Screenshots and Videos."

Capture Duration: To record longer video clips, change how long you hold the Capture Button.

5. Making Use of Screenshot Modes

Press and Hold Capture Button: By depressing the Capture Button, you can take a number of screenshots.

Take Multiple Screenshots: Perfect for recording a series of exciting gameplay scenes.

6. Screenshots Shared on Social Media:

Posting screenshots straight from the album to social media sites connected to your Nintendo account is known as album posting.

Image Editing: Before uploading a screenshot, make simple adjustments, add a caption, and add a filter.

7. distributing video clips:
Album sharing: Publish video straight from the album on other websites or social media.
Twitter Integration: To post gameplay videos with ease, connect your Twitter account.

8. Integration of Amiibo:
Take pictures of your favourite Amiibo figures with the integrated Amiibo Camera.
Customise with Stamps: You can improve screenshots by putting your own overlays and stamps on them.

9. How to Arrange Screenshots:
Make Folders: Group screen grabs for particular games or themes into unique folders.
Album Sorting: Arrange screenshots for quick access by using the game title or capture date.

10. Snapping QR Codes
Scan QR Codes: To find in-game content or promotions, use the Capture Button to scan QR codes.

Compatible Games: QR codes are used in certain games to redeem special items or incentives.

11. Safety and Privacy:

Sensitive Information: Exercise caution when taking screenshots of sensitive information.

Parental Controls: Use these to control the capabilities that allow younger users to take screenshots and record videos.

Using Amiibo Integration to Unlock Adventures on Your Nintendo Switch:

Dive into a realm of interactive gameplay with Amiibo integration on your Nintendo Switch. These adorable figurines allow you to access premium features, extras, and customised gaming experiences in your preferred games by bridging the gap between the real and virtual worlds. Here's how to easily incorporate Amiibo into your gaming adventures:

1. Comprehending Amiibo
Amiibo are collectible figurines and cards that showcase popular characters from Nintendo properties.
Amiibo and your Nintendo Switch can communicate via Near Field Communication (NFC).

2. Games that go well together:
Examine Compatibility: See if an Amiibo is compatible with a particular game.
Amiibo Logo: To determine which games are compatible, look for the Amiibo logo on the box or in-game menus.

3. How to get Amiibo to work:

Joy-Con or Pro Controller: To activate an Amiibo, place it on the appropriate Joy-Con or Pro Controller's NFC touchpoint.

Nintendo Switch Lite: To activate an Amiibo, utilise the standalone Nintendo Switch Pro Controller or an extra Joy-Con.

4. amiibo camera

Album Feature: On your Nintendo Switch, navigate to the Album area to access the Amiibo Camera.

Seize the Moments: Using Amiibo, take imaginative and entertaining pictures with your favourite characters.

5. How to Unlock in-game Content

Strong Boosts: In games that are compatible, Amiibo can offer strong boosts, exclusive outfits, or equipment.

Customising Gameplay: In certain games, you can add Amiibo figures to the virtual environment to make your gaming experience more unique.

6. Connecting Particular Characters using Amiibo:
Binding to Characters: In games that are compatible, Amiibo may need to be bound to particular characters or profiles.
Character Recognition: By identifying the precise Amiibo figure you've connected, the game can provide you with unique experiences.

7. Series of Collectible Cards:
Amiibo Cards: As a collectible and transportable substitute for figurines, certain Amiibo are offered in card form.
Features of Cards: Cards offer in-game bonuses and features, just like miniatures do.

8. Amiibo Challenges and Tournaments:
Special Events: Take part in exclusive in-game competitions, challenges, or events that Amiibo unlocks.
Compete and Work Together: Show off your prowess in unique tasks or work together with Amiibo in cooperative games.

9. Nintendo Switch Online and Amiibo:
Integration with Online Services: A few titles have the ability to combine Amiibo capabilities with online services offered by Nintendo Switch.
Online Competitions: Use Amiibo-enhanced features to compete against other players or against yourself.

10. Amiibo Display and Collection:
Exhibit Your Collection: You can choose to collect and display your Amiibo figures in person or through an in-game display.
Interactive Displays: Some games include interactive displays or virtual showcases for your Amiibo collection.

11. Suitable for Use with Additional Nintendo Devices:
Cross-Device Compatibility: Some Amiibo offer value by being compatible with other Nintendo devices.
Nintendo 3DS: A select number of Amiibo are compatible with Nintendo 3DS systems.

TROUBLESHOOTING AND MAINTENANCE

Set out to repair and manage your Nintendo Switch so that you can play games that work reliably and smoothly. We explore the art of fixing common problems, maximising performance, and extending the life of your console in this area. Come learn the fundamentals of troubleshooting and maintenance, from resolving connectivity issues to preventing future hardware issues. Together, we can help you get over challenges and maintain your Nintendo Switch in top shape so you can play endless games. Greetings from the world of maintenance and troubleshooting, where every obstacle becomes a chance to improve your gaming skills.

Navigating Common Issues and Solutions on Your Nintendo Switch:

Having difficulties with playing games? Do not be alarmed! This book serves as your compass through frequent problems with your Nintendo Switch, offering workable fixes to maintain a fun and seamless gaming experience. Let's solve the problems that may arise, from software bugs to connectivity issues:

1. Connectivity Difficulties:
Wi-Fi problems: Make sure your Switch is in the coverage area of your router and think about changing the channel in your router configuration.
Reduce the number of devices sharing the same Wi-Fi frequency to minimise interference.

2. Issues with Controller Connectivity:
Reconnecting Joy-Cons: You can reconnect Joy-Cons by pressing the Sync button on the side or by fastening them to the console.
Pro Controller Sync: Use a USB cable or the dock to synchronise the Pro Controller.

3. Display and Docking Problems:
To reset the dock, unplug the HDMI and power wires, give it a minute, and then plug them back in. Display Settings: Check System Settings for display settings that work with your TV.

4. Unresponsive or frozen system:
Soft Reset: Press and hold the power button for a minimum of 15 seconds to carry out a soft reset.
Force Shutdown: If necessary, hold down the power button for an extended period of time to force a shutdown.

5. Software Errors or Crashes:
Update your system software and games to the latest versions in order to receive bug patches.
Reinstall Software: If problems continue, try reinstalling the troublesome software.

6. Issues with Charging:
Verify the charging wire to make sure it is firmly attached and undamaged.
Dock Charging: Make sure the dock is operational and correctly connected if you're using one.

7. Problems Reading MicroSD Cards:
Remove and re-insert the microSD card to make sure the connection is made correctly.
Verify Compatibility: Make sure the Switch and the microSD card are compatible.

8. Overheating System:
Ventilation: Make sure the console's vents are not obstructed for adequate ventilation.
Cooling Stand: To avoid overheating during prolonged gaming sessions, use a cooling stand.

9. Joy-Con Divergence:
Adjust the Joy-Cons' calibration in the System Settings to lessen drift problems.
Get in touch with Nintendo Support: If drift continues, get in touch with Nintendo Support for more help.

10. Issues with accounts and online services:
Reset your password to access your Nintendo Account if you are having trouble logging in.
Nintendo Switch Online: Verify the current state of the service to see if there have been any issues reported.

11. Problems with the Bluetooth audio connection:
Verify the compatibility of your Bluetooth headphones or other audio equipment.
Restart Bluetooth: If problems occur, try restarting the Switch or unplugging and reassembling your Bluetooth devices.

12. Lockout of Parental Control:
Reset PIN: Follow the instructions below to reset the PIN if Parental Controls have locked you out.
Support: For help with ongoing problems, get in touch with Nintendo Support.

How to Keep Your Nintendo Switch Clean and Safe:

Maintaining the immaculate state of your Nintendo Switch guarantees excellent performance and prolonged enjoyment. To maintain your console and accessories clean and free from damage, adhere to this guide:

1. Cleaning of the screen:
Microfiber Cloth: To get rid of fingerprints and smudges, gently clean the screen with a microfiber cloth.
Screen Protector: For further security, think about using a film or tempered glass screen protector.

2. External Cleaning:
Wet Cloth: To clean the outside, wet a gentle cloth with water or a light cleaning solution.
Steer Clear of Harsh Chemicals: Steer clear of harsh or abrasive cleaning products that could scratch the surface.

3. Handling Joy-Cons and Controllers:

Soft Brush: To clean dust and dirt out of controller buttons and cracks, use a soft brush or compressed air.

Controller Covers: To prevent spills and scratches, think about getting silicone covers for the Pro Controller and the Joy-Cons.

4. Dock Upkeep:

Dust Removal: To remove any dust from the USB ports on the dock, use a can of compressed air.

Ventilation: To ensure enough ventilation, make sure the dock's vents are unobstructed.

5. Slot and port cleaning:

Canned Air: Use canned air to remove dust from the ports and slots on the console.

Toothpick or Cotton Swab: Use a toothpick or cotton swab to gently clean ports and remove any dirt.

6. Safe Cases:

Hard Shell Cases: To protect your Switch from knocks and impacts, get a hard shell case for travel.

Soft Pouches: For protection while travelling without adding bulk, think about using a soft pouch.

7. Handling Cables:

Cable Ties: To avoid cable tangling and lessen the strain on connectors, use cable ties or organisers.

Prevent Tension: Keep cables from bending at sharp angles to avoid putting tension on them.

8. Solutions for Storage:

Appropriate Storage: Keep your Switch out of direct sunlight and in a cool, dry location.

Avoid Extreme Temperatures: To avoid damaging your console, keep it away from extreme temperatures.

9. Frequent Exams:

Visual Check: Check your Switch on a regular basis for indications of wear, damage, or loose parts.

Button Functionality: Regularly check that the buttons and controls are working properly.

10. Refusing Meals and Drinks:

Food and Drink-Free Zone: To avoid spills, keep food and beverages away from your gaming area.

Cleaning Spills Right Away: If there are any spills, shut off and disconnect your switch right away, then clean up the mess completely.

11. Preventive Maintenance:

Update Software: To get enhanced performance, make sure your games and console are up to date.

Backup Data: Using Nintendo Switch Online or other backup techniques, make regular backups of your save data.

12. Treat with Caution:

Gentle Handling: Don't drop or handle your Switch roughly; instead, treat it with gentle care.

Use Straps: To avoid unintentional drops when playing in portable or tabletop mode, use wrist straps.

UPDATES AND UPCOMING FUNCTIONALITIES

Discover what's in store for your Nintendo Switch in the future by exploring the upgrades and features that are still to come. This section delves into the always changing world of software updates, gaming enhancements, and upcoming exciting features. As we explore the most recent advancements, you can stay ahead of the curve and make sure that your Switch experience is always at the forefront of innovation. Come along with us as we explore the possibilities for upcoming features and improvements that will influence the next installments of your gaming journey. Welcome to the world of updates and upcoming features, where new opportunities are unlocked with each update and where features offer a peek at how the gaming industry is changing.

Navigating System Updates and Patch Notes on Your Nintendo Switch:

Take a trip down memory lane with your Nintendo Switch as we explore system upgrades and the fascinating world of patch notes. This section will help you comprehend the value of updates, interpret patch notes, and remain up to current on the newest features. Let's explore the intricacies of system updates and make sure your Switch is updated and ready for the newest additions and enhancements.

2. The significance of updating systems:

Enhanced Stability: Stability enhancements for the entire system are frequently included in system updates.

Access new features, functions, and optimisations by unlocking them.

Patches for security: Apply patches to your console to keep it safe from potential vulnerabilities.

2. Updates that happen automatically:

Background Downloads: To enable your Switch to download and install updates in the background, turn on automatic updates.

Wi-Fi connected: In order to get automatic updates, make sure your Switch is linked to a Wi-Fi network.

3. Check for Manual Updates:
System Settings: Check the "System" section of the System Settings manually for updates.
Download and Install: To download and install an update, follow the on-screen instructions if one is available.

4. Examining the Patch Notes:
Patch notes: What Are They? Patch notes are comprehensive reports that outline enhancements and modifications that go along with upgrades.
Getting to the Patch Notes: For comprehensive patch notes, check out the News section on your Switch or the official Nintendo website.

5. Comprehending Patch Notes:
Fixes for known problems or bugs in games or system software are listed here.
Explore the latest features, functions, and compatibility enhancements.

Performance Optimisations: Find out about improvements to performance that make things run more smoothly.

6. Updates Specific to a Game:

Patches for specific games: Updates for specific games may be sent apart from system updates.

Game News Section: For updates pertaining to individual games, check out the Game News section on your Switch.

7. Obtaining Updates for Games:

Menu with Game Icons: To check for updates, navigate to the game's icon on the Home Menu.

Download and install game updates to enjoy enhanced gameplay and fresh content.

8. Selecting Beta Releases:

Nintendo Switch Online: Sign up for Nintendo Switch Online to get access to alpha versions of updates and features.

Giving Input: Take part in testing initiatives to offer input on planned enhancements.

9. Make a backup before updating:

Before making any significant modifications, think about utilising Nintendo Switch Online to backup your save data.

Prevent Data Loss: Safeguard your gaming progress in the event that unanticipated problems occur when updating.

10. Upcoming Functions Teasers:

In Patch Notes, teasing Patch notes can occasionally provide hints about new features or upgrades.

Official Declarations: For details on upcoming improvements, pay attention to official announcements.

Looking Forward to New Nintendo Switch Games and Excited Features:

Set off on an exciting voyage of discovery as we examine the features and titles that could improve your Nintendo Switch experience. This section serves as your guide to the highly anticipated features that are almost ready for release and offer intriguing improvements and innovative features. Furthermore, we'll reveal a preview of some of the games that will soon be available on your platform. Come along on the ride of anticipation as we explore the future terrain and get you fired up about what lies ahead for your Nintendo Switch:

1. Improved Internet Resources: Nintendo Switch Online Development It is anticipated that the Nintendo Switch Online service will undergo updates and enhancements, possibly bringing additional features and enhanced functionalities.

   Multiplayer Improvements: Keep an eye out for additions that improve connectivity and the online multiplayer experience.

2. Innovations in Firmware:

Upgrades to System Firmware: Keep an eye out for firmware updates that will include novel features and enhance the Switch's operating system.

Improvements to the User Interface: For a more fluid and intuitive experience, expect UI improvements and tinkering.

3. Retro or Virtual Console Gaming Additions:

Library of Classic Games: Look out for updates on the Virtual Console or additional methods to play old titles.

Vintage Assortments: Anticipate carefully selected sets of beloved games from Nintendo's extensive history of gaming.

4. System Performance Enhancements:

Smoother Performance: To guarantee a more responsive and fluid gaming experience, expect continuous system performance optimisations.

Load Time Improvements: Keep an eye out for updates designed to speed both system and game load times.

5. Cloud Gaming Integration: Examine how cloud gaming services might be integrated to give players access to a wider selection of games.

Streaming additions: Get ready for additions that improve your Switch's ability to stream and play cloud games.

6. Enhanced eShop Functionality:

eShop Upgrades: Be on the lookout for updates to the eShop, which could include additional browsing choices, tailored suggestions, or special offers.

Better Discoverability: Look forward to improvements that facilitate finding and exploring new games and content.

7. Options for Customising the Console: Skins and Themes: Watch for the release of customised skins and themes to add flair to your console's look.

Different Icons: Be prepared for the prospect of tunable icon variants to enable a more customised Home Menu.

8. Game Releases and Sequels: Much Awaited Titles: Get ready for the arrival of much awaited

titles that promise captivating gameplay, stunning graphics, and engrossing storytelling.

Anticipate the release of beloved franchises' sequels and expansions, which will offer new adventures to your Switch.

9. Exclusive Partnerships:

Special Collaborations: Keep an eye out for Nintendo and other creators working together exclusively to deliver games that are distinct and unanticipated.

Limited-Edition material: Keep an eye out for accessories and consoles with themes that are part of limited-edition material related to unique collaborations.

10. Official Reveals: Nintendo Direct Announcements To learn about official announcements about new features, system updates, and game releases, watch Nintendo Direct presentations.

Showcase Events: Keep an eye out for showcase events that will reveal a future roadmap for the Nintendo Switch.

CONCLUSION

We've covered every aspect of your gaming companion as we come to a conclusion with this in-depth guide to your Nintendo Switch. With your newfound knowledge of troubleshooting, exploring advanced features, understanding the fundamentals, and planning ahead, you'll be able to maximise your gaming experience.

Your Nintendo Switch is more than simply a gaming system; it's also a doorway to fascinating journeys, a world of creativity, and a supportive gaming community. Keep in mind that the Switch is a dynamic platform that changes and adapts as you play with game libraries, adjust system settings, and wait for new releases.

You can experience the joy of gaming regardless of your level of experience. The Nintendo Switch is a huge universe with a wide variety of games, special features, and limitless opportunities. I hope your gaming sessions are engrossing, your victories sweet, and your memories everlasting as you explore the plethora of games and features.

Thank you for joining us on this tour of your Nintendo Switch. I hope you have a lot of fun, adventure, and pure joy playing games in the future and being a member of the Nintendo Switch community. Go forth, and may your journeys in the vast world of gaming continue to unfold!

Printed in Great Britain
by Amazon

40744445R00056